BRITAIN'S  HERITAGE

Model Villages

Tim Dunn

AMBERLEY

Acknowledgements

Thank you to my parents, who pushed me to apply to work at Bekonscot as a child. To the staff at Bekonscot (especially Merve) who have indulged me over these years. And to all those who have let me hunt out, talk about, build, question, photograph, pick up, hoard - and obsess over – model villages. I have been lucky to have you. Thank you also to Nick Wright, Derek Smith and Stephen Levrant of Heritage Architecture Ltd, David McKinstry of the Georgian Group, and the many teams and individuals at the various model villages who have assisted me. Thanks for photographic contributions are also due to Brighton Toy & Model Museum, Chris Marchant, Derek Smith, Jan Whitehead, John Hinde Collection, Margate Museum, National Trust and Puffin Books.

First published 2017

Amberley Publishing
The Hill, Stroud
Gloucestershire, GL5 4EP

www.amberley-books.com

Copyright © Tim Dunn, 2017

The right of Tim Dunn to be identified as the Author of this work has been asserted in accordance with the Copyrights, Designs and Patents Act 1988.

ISBN 978 1 4456 6914 4 (paperback)
ISBN 978 1 4456 6915 1 (ebook)

British Library Cataloguing in Publication Data.
A catalogue record for this book is available from the British Library.

Printed in the UK.

Contents

1

Introduction: What Is a Model Village?

Model villages are the work of brilliant minds; frustrated, brilliant minds. For it is often from frustration that the most remarkable sparks of genius fizz into life.

Whether an outsider artist's frustration to realise their utopia, the frustration of a nostalgia seeker trying to hold on to a caricature of the past, or a savvy entrepreneur's frustration at needing to generate profit, model villages, miniature towns and tiny cities have very occasionally been the result. They are works of art; works of art that have been overlooked. Until, perhaps, now.

The model villages of Britain are quirky and varied; they are brilliant and they are a joy. They are compromises, they are struggles, and they are the work of hundreds of thousands of hours' toil. They might often appear delightfully simple, bringing joy, escapism or amusement to the visitor. But each model village represents even greater joy, escapism, amusement or perhaps heartbreak for its creator. Whether built for love, for commercial gain or perhaps for a reason that the originator cannot quite articulate, each model village has a fascinating story to tell.

Some model villages, miniature towns and scaled-down cities are public affairs, intended for the eyes of many, whereas some are private passions, and I have tried to show a few places that we outsiders have probably not yet seen before.

They fall between the cracks of so many splendidly specific obsessions and passions: model railways, dolls' houses and miniatures, gardening, follies, architecture, urban planning, crafts and history. It is because the end result of a model village so often encompasses these established areas of academic or amateur interest – or indeed makes a stab at attempting them all – that a specialist observer might consider a model village impure, naïve, or of no interest whatsoever. These are fabulous hotch-potch mish-mashes of ideas, rarely concluding

To wander around a model village or town, such as the one at Wimborne in Dorset, can often feel like visiting a completely new world.

in the way they were conceived. They are just as any real town might be: envisioned, varied and evolved, a palimpsest.

But they are not real towns, of course. The term 'model village' can also be applied to a real planned settlement, such as Titus Salt's great Saltaire, or Cadbury's compact Bournville. Set out as utopias by those who held power, these places are fascinating and they are model in concept but not, apart from maybe Portmeirion in Wales, quite in the scope of this book.

Some people (most people) stop making models quite young. Some people (most people) stop making models when they tire of washing-up-bottles, PVA glue and bits of cardboard. But some people – wonderful, intriguing people – continue. They build; they create.

The model village concept has proliferated in Britain and that is where this book has its focus, but the British are not alone in their love of tiny worlds. The USA, Germany and Japan are other nations with mild miniature obsessions, for reasons of space and craftsmanship in the latter and very much model railways in the former two.

Mr & Mrs Abrahams in Shawcross, Hampshire, constructed a unique town from tiny home-fired bricks. They cast them in matchboxes: note the sign welcoming donations of empty matchboxes.

Tucktonia, in Dorset. Britain's largest ever model village was a remarkable landscape full of landmark buildings, but it lasted only ten years.

A model is a three-dimensional representation of something, and a village in the traditional sense can be considered anything from a couple of buildings to a town. Model villages – or miniature towns – are often found outdoors, whereas scale cities are generally found indoors. There is something simple and appropriate about lumpy vernacular buildings, built from 'traditional' materials sitting in a flower bed. It is rather more tricky to build a modernist skyscraper from readily available household and garden materials, so they are usually constructed more finely, and often find themselves displayed as cityscapes indoors.

Many models of villages are found indoors and as the scope of this book is broad, we will take in a couple of indoor landscapes along the way. Let us not draw too many borders, because they blur quickly, and it is where things meet that the most interesting things occur.

There is a variation in scale, too; anything from the chunky 1:9 of Bourton-on-the-Water to the 1:76 of Pendon Museum. The majority are what eminent heritage architect and model village enthusiast Stephen Levrant calls 'Gulliver' style; that is they are walk-through landscapes outdoors where you can in many cases touch the buildings. They are the real Lilliputs. Others are less cohesive landscapes, rather like parkland, with models on display individually. To some, these aren't true model villages. A model village generally has to be a collection of buildings – rather than say, just a single windmill by a pond – and there are more often than not model people, or landscapes or transport. A proper scene, in miniature.

But if someone, at some point, has conceived it as a model village, and if visitors call it a model village, it is probably a model village. I hope that this book encourages you to look at model villages again, and to make a visit.

Let us explore.

Did you know?

The Scope of a Model Village is Broad
As long as it's a model, as long as it has some sort of scale (even if it is not consistent), and as long as it's more than one or two buildings, it's probably a model village.

The author exploring Britain's oldest intact model village: Bekonscot, in Buckinghamshire. (Credit: Chris Marchant)

2
Where Did It All Begin?

Our journey back in time and down in scale begins properly, perhaps surprisingly, in Japan. Maybe it is not a coincidence that two of the nations who fetishise the concept of miniaturisation most are those which are small, densely populated islands with an often frenetic pace of life and an occasional unease about their pace of progress.

Throughout history the idea of miniaturising something either as a replica, or as a concept – created small because of limited resources or to make it practical – is well documented. From the most simple of children's toys to replica items pushed into pharaohs' tombs to accompany them in the afterlife, miniatures are a worldwide phenomenon.

But it is in Japan where widespread evidence of miniature landscapes and something more comprehensively planned than a single object is to be found. Way back in the year 612 the Empress Suiko had a garden built with an artificial mountain depicting Mount Sumeru, reputed in Hindu and Buddhist legends to be located at the centre of the world. One of her ministers had a garden built at his palace featuring a lake with several small islands, representing the islands of the Eight Immortals famous in Chinese legends and Daoist philosophy. Tiny bonsai trees and roadways proliferated and such gardens became popular for the next thousand years. As they developed, bridges, rocks and temples would be erected to represent something far larger, and these 'promenade gardens' were widely popular.

It was not until the eighteenth century that the prevailing mood was ready to embrace this form of landscaping in Britain. Japanese culture had begun to be transported to the West, and the formality of the early Georgian period had begun to give way to the constructed landscapes of Capability Brown. These were full-size model landscapes.

It was in the mid-nineteenth century that alpine areas began to appear as fashionable adjuncts to gardens. Ferneries and dells became popular in private gardens of the wealthy and little 'fairy glens' appear in pleasure gardens by the late 1890s. The Victorian at repose had not just the wherewithal to fund a garden, but also that to visit other gardens too.

The rock garden probably drove the early miniature landscaping in British gardening: tiny gorges, pathways and house-like lanterns were common. By 1881 Kew Gardens had created a grand fern rockery, but perhaps most astonishing is that seen at Friar Park, near Henley, in Oxfordshire. Here a great alpine garden in a very large rockery was constructed – topped by a miniature Matterhorn mountain. Below it, tiny cast iron goats were positioned. This is not a child's farm; this was for adults to observe and enjoy on their promenade, and enjoy it they did. In the hands of Beatle George Harrison it was restored. The peak remains.

Indoor model trains (for children of wealthy families), developed initially as 'dribblers' with steam and water spilling out, puffed around on the floor, often with no track. These had now become more widely available and firms like Bing of Germany and Bassett-Lowke of the UK were selling thousands of model railway sets, ostensibly on the floor.

A postcard of the Alpine Gardens at Friar Park, Henley. A pair of climbers have been added to the landscape to the left of the 'Matterhorn', faking the perspective. Scale animals were also to be seen.

MINIATURE TABLE RAILWAY.

An early model table-top model railway as sold in Britain before the First World War. Aside from model building sets, farms and soldiers, these were the earliest examples of controllable worlds being made available for purchase – and for imaginations to disappear into.

As middle-class wealth grew, so did their trainsets. These trainsets had to go outdoors, because they wouldn't fit indoors. Occasionally, an outdoor scale model railway was seen by the early 1900s, but these were rarely in landscapes that extended far beyond the railway lineside. In 1910 Mr W. W. Morrice described his double-track ground-level garden railway in *Model Railways and Locomotives Magazine* as being something quite special, but there were few buildings. There was no interest in the surrounding landscape for model railway enthusiasts; they didn't want to play town planner, architect, or Capability Brown. They wanted to play trains.

It was not until modellers such as Edward Beale and John Aherne (whose great work 'The Madder Valley Railway' is preserved at Pendon Museum in Oxfordshire) started to write about model landscapes and miniature building construction that comprehensive model railway scenery began. Still, with improved production techniques enabling models to be built commercially – and improved education to enable better comprehension of the world – children could start to lay model buildings, farms and villages on the floor. Wooden, kit and even tiny ceramic buildings covered carpets. There were models for war planning, models to remember places and models to demonstrate. On holiday, gnome and fairy gardens started to appear in seaside resort towns: miniature worlds, fantasy worlds. Utopias.

People now had money, education, media to inspire and, crucially, leisure time. They had the ability to visualise frustrations or desires in their heads; it all pours out and people start to craft with their hands. A fire is lit and it explodes with the most remarkable result: modelmaking.

The first recorded true model village in Britain was in Hampstead, London, at the private home of Charles Paget Wade. Wade, a passionate collector of great means and with more than a passing interest in architecture, created the 1:24 scale Fladbury around the edge of the garden in 1908. It was complete, of course, with a 1:32 scale

Right: Bassett-Lowke's advertising suggested much more than just the model trains. The dream was depicted: a railway empire, a subordinated landscape, built and operated by a young emperor in his own back garden.
Below: Central to the dream of the ultimate model railway was the taming of one of the icons of the age: *Flying Scotsman*. (Brighton Toy & Model Museum)

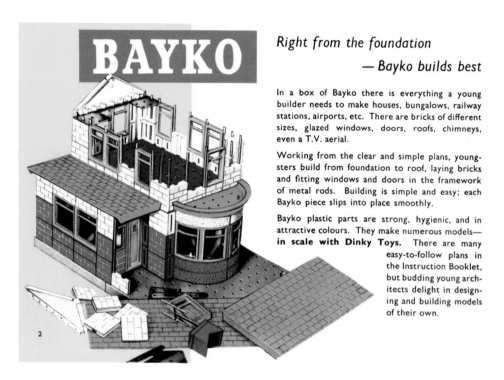

BAYKO

Right from the foundation
— Bayko builds best

In a box of Bayko there is everything a young builder needs to make houses, bungalows, railway stations, airports, etc. There are bricks of different sizes, glazed windows, doors, roofs, chimneys, even a T.V. aerial.

Working from the clear and simple plans, youngsters build from foundation to roof, laying bricks and fitting windows and doors in the framework of metal rods. Building is simple and easy; each Bayko piece slips into place smoothly.

Bayko plastic parts are strong, hygienic, and in attractive colours. They make numerous models— **in scale with Dinky Toys.** There are many easy-to-follow plans in the Instruction Booklet, but budding young architects delight in designing and building models of their own.

here's a fascinating new game

MODEL MAKING

Above: Although from after the First World War, Bayko is an example of a popular building toy. Like Meccano, these were hands-on toys that enabled children to miniaturise the world around them and make sense of it on their own terms. (Brighton Toy & Model Museum)
Left: There were many make-it-yourself model village books: this one accompanied cut-out card buildings with Quaker Oat packets. Before the age of *Minecraft* and *SimCity* computer games, these were the simulations of their day.

Did you know?

An Ecumenical Matter?
Trips from the UK to Italy brought back ideas of grottoes, established there for many years. Catholic shrines also occasionally had remarkable, but usually tightly constrained, miniature town representations often focusing on Bethlehem.

Likely the first picture of a documented 'proper' model village in Britain, dating from *c.* 1908: Charles Wade's original layout at Hampstead, West London. (National Trust)

A later drawing of the full Wolf's Cove as laid out at Snowshill in the 1930s, as depicted in the Puffin book *Marvellous Models* by W. Bassett-Lowke. (Puffin Books)

(gauge 1) Bassett-Lowke model railway. A move to Snowshill Manor in Gloucestershire saw the buildings and model railway move with him. There it was rearranged in the form of Wolf's Cove, a Cornish fishing village, around the edge of a miniature harbourside contrived from a fish pond. The buildings were loosely arranged with accessories and a working canal: they were taken in each autumn for protection. Word spread and it appeared in various news and review publications in the 1920s.

After Wade's death, Snowshill Manor was taken over by the National Trust, and eventually the village was retired to be displayed indoors along with Wade's other collections.

Elsewhere, Mrs Pulestone, a rare female instigator, constructed a 1:12 scale model in her garden in about 1927; cottages, a pond and farm were supplemented by a Bassett-Lowke model railway. Very possibly inspired by Wade's Snowshill model, a Pathé newsreel of the time shows her painting models for the camera, guests strolling about the scene and even smoke wafting out of tiny chimneys. A bucolic scene and one that likely did not last long, but along with Snowshill – not a million miles from the Buckinghamshire home of wealthy accountant Roland Callingham – it may well have provided an ignition spark for the now world-famous Bekonscot.

Bekonscot is located in the Metroland town of Beaconsfield. Here, Roland Callingham had previously set out areas including a fern dell, formal rose gardens and Japanese pagoda-style lanterns. According to a 1931 *Daily Sketch* article, a few small buildings had been laid out in what was known as the 'Swiss Garden', and a model railway of 1,200 feet followed soon after. Callingham himself notes that no overall plan was adhered to, but his friend James Shilcock developed the Gauge 1 railway, had track parts and stock supplied by Bassett-Lowke and was ably assisted by Callingham's house staff and local contractors. The railway really was the centrepiece, with automatic signalling and a huge collection of electrically powered engines.

Callingham lived in Beaconsfield, Shilcock was from Ascot; so it was that the portmanteau Bekonscot was created. Maryloo, the main terminus, was a crashing together of Marylebone

1928: the main town of Bekonscot begins to take shape around the rockeries, with the remains of the old garden rapidly disappearing in the background.

The year before Bekonscot opened to the public, the only visitors were friends and colleagues of its creator Roland Callingham. In this hitherto unseen 1928 view, visitors holding tennis racquets prior to a game are pictured in the main town. The village was later extended across the tennis courts.

A never-before-seen view of Bekonscot's creator, Roland Callingham (left), and head gardener Tom Berry (right) during an early rebuild of the main model railway terminus, Maryloo.

and Waterloo: the two London stations to which the gentlemen each commuted. This was not a village, railway and landscape intended for public view, but for private entertainment. It is said that Callingham was occasionally found to be swimming in his 'sea' even into the years when it was open to the public. Well, it was his garden, after all.

And what a village that early Bekonscot was. Cascading over a rockery that enclosed the swimming pool on three sides, it was broadly of 1:12 scale, although by his own admission, Callingham was 'prepared to sacrifice exact scale for the right effect'. Conifers were shaped to look like oak trees and the architecture was crude (often in hewn stone with wood) but it was still utterly delightful. He commissioned the celebrated artist Edmund Dulac to create tiny stained glass windows for the minster church, and a local electrician to install hundreds of tiny lamps. His head gardener Tom Berry (forever immortalised in the name of the first castle he constructed, Bekonberry) was the driving force behind much of the building

1931: the gates to Bekonscot are opened, and the model village story really begins.

but Callingham took an active role too. This was gardening, modelmaking and building construction on a scale only a team could tackle. Two of those early gardening hands were still working for Bekonscot at the turn of the twenty-first century, displaying some of the dedication and loyalty that a passionate project such as Bekonscot can engender.

1930 was a warm year. During the long summer evenings, Callingham and his wife hosted garden parties and tennis matches on the courts adjoining the main lake. Drifting from the serious business of gin, small-talk and tennis balls, guests were entranced by dragonflies skipping over tiny fields, miniature lamps glistening in the gloam and the clicking of tiny train wheels through the forest. Those lucky few requested that others should be privileged to see such a remarkable sight – so between his days leading his accountancy firm, Callingham charged his household team to add more buildings and expand the pathways. In early 1931 the gates were flung open, donations for charity were taken by means of a house with a slot in the roof, the press arrived and the world gawped, with eyes wide-open.

Did you know?

The World's Oldest?
Bekonscot is known to many as the world's oldest model village, an epithet gained in the 1970s probably because few knew any different. Given the continued existence of Wolf's Cove at Snowshill, and the survival of 1:6 scale 'Tiny Town' in Colorado, that title is not entirely accurate – but perhaps in the spirit of fun it can continue. After all, both Tiny Town and Wolf's Cove spent many years in the wilderness and have little of their original village as part of the display.

3
Fame and Fortune

Bekonscot was the surprise smash hit that didn't even try to chart. A whimsical product of the time, it was welcome respite for those weary of Pathé newsreels, *Daily Sketch* and *Standard* coverage of strikes and international unrest. Here was something novel, something weird, something new. A 'real life Lilliput... with all modern amenities' said the *Illustrated London News*; it was a human story of middle-class utopia realised – and just outside London, so journalists didn't have to go too far. Right by the station and near to the pub, too.

I mentioned in my opening gambit that every model village is the result of frustration. Roland Callingham's domestic frustration was released by taking his train set outside and building Bekonscot. Back over in the Cotswolds, just a few miles from Snowshill Manor, there was a pub landlord in Bourton-on-the-Water whose frustration was the need for more custom. One Mr Morris needed to differentiate his pub from several others in the popular tourist town. Probably aware of Bekonscot's popularity, and quite likely aware of Wolf's Cove at Snowshill, Morris envisioned a 'miniature mountain glen with hills and river and waterfalls' to add to the pub garden. To complete the scene, 1:9 scale models of the town's picturesque bridges over the River Windrush were cut from local stone, followed by a model of the village hall. By the end of 1936, his ambitions had grown; Morris employed several contractors to measure out the entire core of Bourton's full-size town and had it rebuilt in the same local Cotswold stone, 1:9 scale, at 90 degrees to the prototype in his pub back garden. 'It enables our American cousins to see Bourton-on-the-Water nine times more quickly,' said Morris.

The results are wonderful. The attention to detail is astonishing and the craftsmanship in stone almost unsurpassed in Britain's model villages. Golden stone glows in the sun; the intrepid visitor can skip down wide streets or narrow alleys. The Windrush bridges take the weight of us giant invaders; if we should wish to shrink down and see this tiny Bourton then we can use the rotating periscope at the end of the High Street to get a ground-eye view. It is a magical place, with the large scale buildings often coming above waist height – and the most recent owners, Julian and Vicki, have embarked on an ambitious restoration programme. More of that in Chapter 6.

London has never been a hotbed of model village action – for two reasons. Historically it has been a place people go to experience the contemporary, rather than to escape it; those visiting have quite enough thrills in the 1:1 scale world. And land has been expensive, so laying out little towns to wander around is really quite a costly folly. In the past a few other early villages have existed in and around the capital, but quite small in size, such as 'Lilliput Garden', a collection of very competently built wood-and-concrete landmarks and crazy golf, plus a tiny wooden village in Woolmer Green, Hertfordshire, in a garden known as 'The Woodcarver'. Here, from 1938 hundreds of, well, wood-carved objects adorned the house and garden, and became the subject of many a newsreel. Outsider-art most certainly, scaled they were not, but carved with love indeed.

Less than for love but more for war, a great number of 'villages' – more often than not crude outdoor landscapes – were built by the MOD for training across many sites but few remains exist today.

A splendidly dandy Gulliver strides over Bourton's model village and gasps in surprise. Inside this guidebook he is shown talking to the village's owner, thus self-legitimising the connection to the Swift novel.

Almost real. The winter sun rises in 2017 over Bourton-on-the-Water. Still solid in Cotswold stone, in low light and with no other visitors present, it is quite mesmerising.

From 1943 four delightfully simple Tudor(ish) villages were built in central London, all by one man – Edgar Wilson. This kind Edgar of West Norwood built them during the Second World War from bits of brick, scrap and concrete, displaying a few houses in his front garden. Selflessly and beautifully, he donated three to the people of London via the LCC and they were displayed for war-weary children's enjoyment in Vauxhall, Brockwell and Finsbury Parks.

A fourth, the most wonderful, he donated to people on the other side of the world. This became the Tudor Model Village of Fitzroy Gardens, Melbourne; a tiny town born of the unbridled aching gratitude of that one man. The plaque in the restored village still reads today: 'This Tudor Model Village was presented to the City of Melbourne by the citizens of Lambeth, England, in appreciation of gifts of food dispatched from Victoria to England during food shortages following World War 2.' One of the team who restored the village in 2001 said: 'It looks to me like Wilson must have had some sort of trade background. Although the work is naïve and clumsy, some of it is fairly complicated. But what I really got was a deep sense of the man himself. It's obvious that he'd put his heart and soul into it.'

East of London, the village at Canvey Island, built in the 1940s by Mr John Fenwick, had models of various Canvey Island scenes preserved 'for all time' outdoors plus a rather splendid outdoor O Gauge model railway. Not content with Canvey, Fenwick was also behind the very similar village at Felixstowe, which opened in 1959. Despite having over 53,000 visitors in the first year, it lasted only a few seasons.

Felixstowe did not last long: arranged in a rather geometric setting, there was not much to inspire the casual visitor looking for escapism.

Fred Slaymaker's 'Wonder Village' began life in Sutton near Croydon but relocated with him to Polegate. The entire village was made from scraps and cast-offs by Fred, who is seen proudly here in the centre.

The 1953 Coronation was celebrated in miniature at Fred's village in Polegate, East Sussex. It's rare for there to be temporary displays like this, but Babbacombe in Devon has in recent times made miniature versions of real-life events such as the Great British Bake-Off.

Several small villages built in private, but given wider acclaim, started to appear just as the war ended. Former postal worker Fred Slaymaker built a collection of houses, windmills, castles and streets at his home in Sutton, Surrey – and later moved it to be 'Fred Slaymaker's Wonder Village' in Polegate, Surrey. Such was the proliferation of model villages that a Pathé News report introduced Fred's with an exasperated, 'Oh dear, oh dear. A model village. Another model village...'

It was through mass media and literature that model villages gained fame, and perhaps found some of their inspiration. *Gulliver's Travels* (Jonathan Swift, 1726) in particular has a lot to answer for. His Lilliput has been referenced umpteen times in model villages, but occasionally it is a model village that forms the story itself. Enid Blyton lived adjacent to Bekonscot for many years, asking, 'Would you like to come with me and visit a village so small that you will tower above the houses?' in her 1951 book about the place, *The Enchanted Village*.

Mary Norton lived not far away and in 1961 published *The Borrowers Aloft*, in which the tiny protagonists live in a model village, Little Fordham. Norton's Little Fordham is clearly based on the story of Bekonscot; both real and fantasy villages were run by kindly old gentlemen who opened their villages to collect charity donations for the Railway Benevolent

And then, of course, John sees the miniature railway!

"Look!" he says, struck with delight. "LOOK! Bekonscot has even got its own railway!"

It certainly has. How are the tiny folk of Bekonscot to get about if they have no railway? And then we hear the rumble-rattle-rumble of a coming train, and we stand still to see it race past on its track, carriages and all.

"It's stopping at the station!" says John. So it is. Then we hear a second rumbling and another train goes by at our feet, on the other track. And wherever we go in this tiny village we see the trains rattling and racing round the miniature countryside. It makes it all very, very real.

Each train eventually arrives at the big terminus of Maryloo – what a thrill to see them rushing in! There is always a crowd of boys watching there – and fathers too!

We wander all round the enchanted village. What things we see!

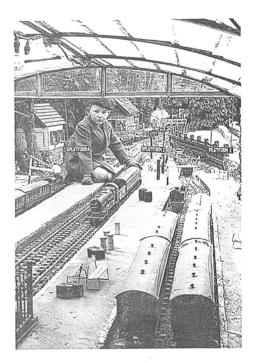

An excerpt from a reprint of Enid Blyton's *The Enchanted Village* set at Bekonscot. The thrill of a tiny train running under one's feet has not abated, many decades on.

Fund. Both real and fantasy villages had a former employee leave and open a commercially focused rival; in the case of Bekonscot this was Stan DeBoo creating several (see page 26).

Fast-forwarding a little out of sync from this book's chronological pattern, the BBC TV adaptation of *The Borrowers* (1993) had a complete model village set created: only one building survived and the author now has this in his collection. For children, Nicholas Fisk's *The Model Village* and Fleur Hitchcock's *Shrunk!* feature full-size people being reduced to fit in existing model villages, while Will Self's collection of adult short stories *Scale* includes a drug-induced miniaturised exploration of Bekonscot. Both Will and Fleur have confessed their adoration of model villages and that is clear from their writing.

On radio, BBC Radio 4's *Robin & Wendy's Wet Weekends* (2001–5) feature a hapless couple who focus their energies on building Mayfield, a model village in their garage, and in the theatre, *Get Ken Barlow* (2005) focused on a kidnap plot involving that *Coronation Street* character, but dealt with people working in a model village kindly. 'These people have found something, something that gets them through this sometimes precarious and harsh thing called life,' said the playwright Ian Kershaw.

Many model villages have hosted various TV shows over the years, but Bekonscot, with its proximity to London, has been especially popular. In one episode of *Midsomer Murders*, a character was killed and tied down Gulliver-like; in the credits of *Dame Edna's Neighbourhood Watch* she skips through the main town looking into windows; and in BBC2's *One Foot In The Past* Bekonscot featured heavily in the credits too. Sitcom *Dad*

(1999) featured George Cole: it was filmed half at Bekonscot and half in a studio set resembling the main railway signal box with trains whizzing through it.

Surely the most famous of all media appearances of model villages must be either the literal destruction of Tucktonia in *Life Force* (1985) or a village built specifically as a film set for *Hot Fuzz* (2001), based on Wimborne Model Town with a bit of real-life Wells thrown in. This film contains the immortal line: 'You wanna be a big cop in a small town? Fuck off up the model village.' Indeed, who could contest that?

During the Second World War, Bekonscot did its bit for Home Front propaganda by staging several scenes to make the headlines. 'Tiny Town Too!' went the headlines accompanying the tin-helmeted head gardener and builder of many structures, Tom Berry.

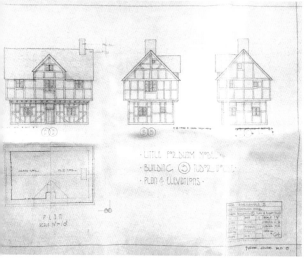

Designers' drawings from the making of a full-size model of a model village: that of Little Ford model village from the BBC TV adaptation of *The Borrowers*. Many model village creators sketch plans before construction for approval and to assist construction, especially necessary for a TV show.

After the war, a model of the *Queen Mary* is seen being readied for refloating in the 'sea'. It would be many times too large for Bekonscot if it matched the 1:12 scale of the Bekonscot docks.

4
Time to Shine: Years in the Sun

During the postwar years, Britain regained its ability to enjoy life. There may have been rationing, but people had time and, crucially, a frustration with being at home so they ventured as far as resources enabled. That often meant the seaside. This was the era of the holiday camp and deckchair, excursion train and picnic. Entrepreneurs started to make the most of it.

Polperro in Cornwall was the first seaside village, opening in 1948. Built as a chunky replica of the town, it tumbled along the road in a garden, with concrete buildings almost all painted white giving a Mediterranean feel as one walks up the narrow paths. It remains open to this day, despite floods and the ever-present threat of concrete degradation, and it is splendid.

The burghers of Wimborne, Dorset, saw the success of Bourton-on-the-Water and wanted a piece of the action. By 1951 a complete 1:10 scale model of Wimborne, constructed entirely from concrete but an almost perfect replica of the local streets (in which you can still wander today) was opened, and very popular it was too. Like Bourton, the buildings are often above waist height – and every shop front was made in wood with details – making it a quite immersive experience. Mr T. Salter, the project lead, was said to be 'extremely cross if you call his enterprise a village'. Wimborne is a town, after all.

In 1954, Mr Arthur Durston built a small collection of houses in Woodstock, Oxfordshire. Woodstock is famous not just for its prettiness or proximity to Blenheim Palace, but also as the town of Mallingford in the 1953 Ealing comedy *The Titfield Thunderbolt*. Again, not a million miles from either Snowshill, Bourton or Bekonscot, Durston saw the value of charging a few pence for tourists to have a look at the model of his hometown, made

You will be captivated by the *Magic* of

THE MODEL VILLAGE AT POLPERRO

An early handbill for Polperro in Cornwall, showing almost the full width of this narrow, but complete, scale model of the town in which it is sited.

The reconstruction of Wimborne Model Town. The 1:10 scale town was sliced apart into chunks of concrete wall and moved several hundred yards to a new site when the original plot was threatened.

A postcard of the church at Skegness, which really does look rather like the one at Southsea.

in stone. In 1992 it was donated by Durston's widow to Blenheim Palace and now it is being restored on display there, a tiny version of the town that sits just outside the palace walls.

Southsea and Skegness need to be mentioned in the same breath, mainly because they are virtually the same thing. While the sites are quite different (Southsea was constructed first, right by the seafront in an old fortress), its creator left soon after the 1956 opening, taking most of the 1:16 scale concrete moulds with him. Arriving in Skegness he saw an opportunity, recast most of the buildings and lo, by 1962 that town had its model village too. Both Southsea and Skegness have been much restored in recent years, and seem to be on track to survive yet.

The Isle of Wight, that island-off-an-island, seems to be such a microcosm of all things archetypically Little England that it inspired Julian Barnes's 1998 novel *England, England*. In

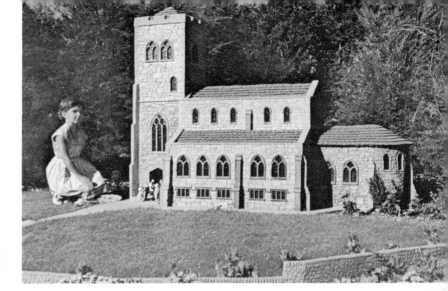

Southsea is a remarkable survivor. Local volunteers like Anne are now assisting the new owners with restoration work, bringing it back to its 1962 glory.

Niton's Buddle Inn had several Isle of Wight landmarks on a miniature concrete island: this view shows it before a model farm and Bembridge Windmill was added.

this the island declares independence and sets itself up as a kind of compressed-England-in-miniature; it will come as no surprise that the island has in real life had at least four model villages and indeed contains the only real village in Britain to have two competing model villages.

The first was in the forecourt of the Buddle Inn in nearby Niton. A small collection of no more than a few yards across laid out in the island's diamond shape, and demolished entirely around 2007, its place has now been taken by wooden decking. I last saw the cracked-up buildings as they sat adjacent to the pub wall; I couldn't get time off work to pick up the last remains that were offered to me. Thus it was that the Buddle Inn's miniature town passed into our collective memory.

In 1952 the first of the two 'competing' model villages began – in Godshill – in the grounds of the Old Vicarage. How terribly, terribly, English. This model village has become one of the greats of the model village world, if there is such a thing. It was developed further in the 1960s by another family, who still own the site and continue to add models of island architecture. At the large scale of 1:10 (matched only by Wimborne), the models are pleasingly tactile, built from timber and concrete; some even have thatched roofs. The tiny population is a particular joy: if anything comes close to the artistry of a sculptor then it is the tiny folk of Godshill. I am reliably informed by Penny Dyer, one the current owners, that all have been created by one talented member of the team with an eye for a character. There are dozens of perfectly placed cameos, each with gentle wit.

Literally across the road from the Old Vicarage is the Old Smithy, a shopping emporium with a walled garden. In this is contained a model shaped as the island – predictably, with various island landmarks. The latter almost seems to try to ambush you as you make your way from the main car park to the 'main' village and, while it is a pleasant garden with nice decoration, has nothing on the 'main' Godshill Model Village.

Godshill in Godshill. A very competent model of the village in which the model is located.

A few model villages of their village have a model village of the model village in them. Godshill, pictured, has a model of the model of the model, which makes it 1:1,000 scale.

The large scale of Godshill has enabled the resident artist to create a remarkably characterful population. They are all unique, crafted in clay.

The last island model village to cover is the most tragic: it fell off a cliff. Now, Blackgang Chine is one of the most wonderful sort of theme parks: one that has no real theme apart, perhaps, from its sheer bonkersness. A collection of various ephemera, buildings, zones and attractions, it was slipping into the Atlantic well before proprietor Alexander Dabell opened the area to the public in 1843. The site has been improved for generations of tourists since, including reproduction smugglers' caves, water gardens, a Tyrannosaurus Rex singing along in the style of Noel Coward, and of course, the addition of a model village in 1953.

This village had models of various island landmarks: Ryde Pier, Osborne House, Godshill's picturesque cluster of thatched cottages (as also seen at Godshill Old Smithy and Godshill Old Vicarage), among others. Its clifftop position, while magnificent, was to be its undoing. With a gradual modernisation of Blackgang Chine and a catastrophic landslip in 1994, the

Did you know?

Pendon, the Masterpiece in Miniature
While outside builders must contend with storms, sun, cats and feet, indoors perfection in almost hermetically sealed environments can be attained. Roye England started to depict his vision of 1930s rural England in great detail: his 4 mm to 1 ft vision has been continued in an Oxfordshire barn by dedicated volunteers for years since.

model village area quite literally disappeared down that cliff. I am assured by the Dabell family that more than a few models still exist in storage, so perchance it is not dead, but sleepeth.

Moving inland, one of the most important cultural events of the immediate postwar era occurred in 1951: the Festival of Britain. While more akin to a set than a true wander-through model village, a huge 'Seaside Town' display was made as a scale model at the Southbank exhibition site; the model village lasted only as long as the exhibition did.

Bekonscot had a narrow escape at this time, too. A 1956 court case tested Callingham, its creator – against people who had moved into homes that now surrounded this once almost rural site – but he and his team won and his life's work survived.

It was Bekonscot, as so often, that provided the launchpad for the two great model village empires: that of Stan Deboo, and that of the Dobbins Brothers. Stan Deboo was the man who made his hobby his profession. 'Ever since I was old enough to carve my initials on the dining room table I have been interested in carving and model making,' he said to *Meccano Magazine*'s reporter in 1963. 'At the ages of thirteen I was very fortunate in being given the opportunity of working with the late Roland Callingham, who designed and built the first [sic] model village in the world.' Deboo was a prolific creator: frustrated perhaps by the lack of commerciality at Bekonscot (indeed, Deboo worked at the NatWest Bank where the Bekonscot account was held), he took the Bekonscot building method of concrete and stone over timber frame inserts to the coast.

He went first to Ramsgate in 1953, where he collaborated with a local entrepreneur to realise a cash-cow which lasted half a century. Few buildings were models of real ones – allowing Deboo to run riot with his ideas. Once Ramsgate was instigated, Deboo then moved on to build Hastings and 'Little Britain' in Weston-super-Mare, both in that by-now popular and handy imperial 1:12-to-1:18-ish scale.

Maintenance at Bekonscot the miniature way.

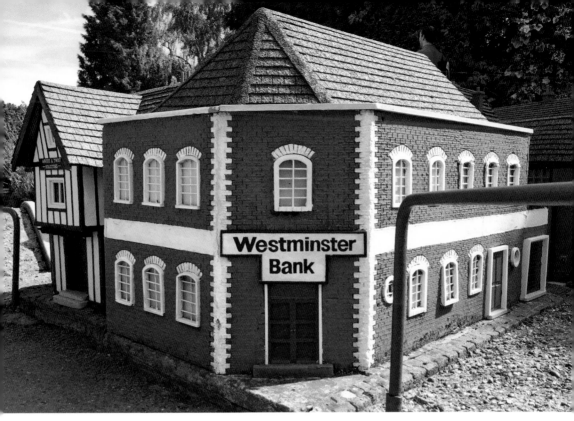

At Bekonscot, the Westminster Bank is 'inspired' by NatWest in Beaconsfield. Coincidentally, this NatWest bank was also where former Bekonscot modelmaker Stan Deboo first worked, before he left to set up Ramsgate, Hastings and Weston-super-Mare villages.

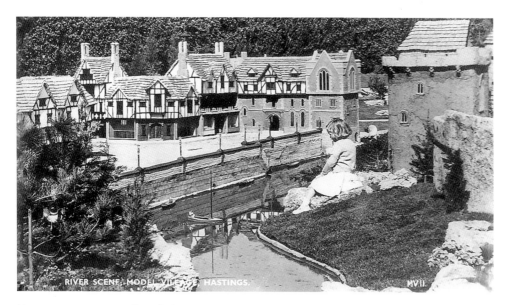

Hastings was exceptionally well designed: like that at Eastbourne, it featured wide paths, a Tudor-style town centre and very competent landscaping. It was a complete region in miniature, but didn't have any moving models to really intrigue young minds.

This Ramsgate jigsaw puzzle, along with other souvenirs such as badges, spoons, coasters, mug and postcards, was a great way to make extra money from the fleeting visitor.

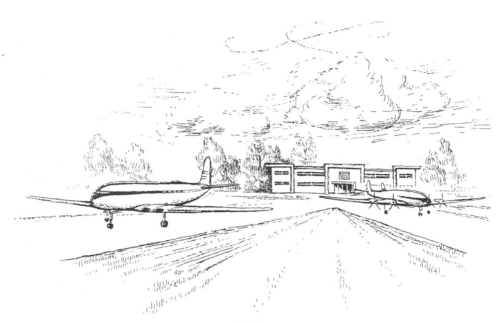

THE AIRPORT

One of the many lovely line drawings of Ramsgate penned by A. R. Bennet. A Comet airliner is seen here at the airport: this building was one of three modernist delights that existed on the same foundations and another is shown in this postcard view with the gyrocopter.

THE MODEL VILLAGE, WEST CLIFF, RAMSGATE   RMV 4

Little Britain, 'The Charm of all England', took four years to build and was proudly electrically lit when in 1962 it opened complete, as all Deboo's sites did, with a published backstory for its inhabitants. Little Britain's was the story of Compton Fiddlestix, Deboo presenting each guidebook as if it were a guide to a real town. He once wrote to me from his home near Battle, Sussex, just a few years before his death. 'It gives me great pleasure,' he said, 'to have written a best-seller.' Over the years, his charming guidebooks must have sold well over 100,000 copies.

The village's little shops and businesses contained some quite awful puns but, like Ramsgate and Hastings, had inspired landscaping and town planning contrived to give enchanting views from almost any angle: these were villages designed to be consumed

THE VILLAGE OF COMPTON FIDDLESTIX

OPEN ALL THE YEAR

LITTLE BRITAIN
MODEL VILLAGE

A 'MUST' FOR YOUR VISIT TO THE WEST COUNTRY

The Charm of all England in half an acre of beautifully landscaped Rock and Water Gardens

'The Charm of all England', depicted in this early advert view of Weston-super-Mare.

62555 · THE CONTEMPORY HOUSE, LITTLE BRITAIN MODEL VILLAGE, WESTON-SUPER-MARE.

'The contemporary house' at Little Britain, Weston-super-Mare, was a rare modernist creation: as far as we know this delightfully visionary building was not based on a full-size example.

by the paying public. But what is truly fascinating about Little Britain is that the fifty buildings over half an acre – 'a composite picture of all that is best in architecture in rural Britain' – were laid out not by Deboo himself, but a woman of great talent – Jacqueline Saunders. Saunders, after four years' study at Birmingham Art College, turned her hand to modelmaking. So here, in an era of male domination in town planning and architecture, we have a rare example of where a woman with great vision and skill has had the authority to lay

Right: A handbill for the first model village at Southport: 'For all Those who are Young In Heart'. The Dobbins brothers commissioned similar artwork for their other villages in Torquay and Great Yarmouth.
Below: Buildings at Southport such as the suspension bridge, town hall and rural village cluster were also to be found at the later Babbacombe in Torquay.

MERRIVALE

PROMENADE **MODEL VILLAGE** SOUTHPORT

OPEN EVERY DAY - ILLUMINATIONS FROM DUSK

The rural idyll was perpetuated. At Southport's Land of the Little People (also known as Merrivale, like Great Yarmouth) visitors came not to see a replica of their town, from which they had escaped for a week, but a dream into which they could drop, albeit briefly.

A country home with a young visitor for scale: this was a popular publicity shot for both Babbacombe and Southport in the 1960s.

out a complete town – an essay in architectural history dressed up as entertainment – for the holidaymaker.

Weston-super-Mare's miniature world was clearly designed by someone more literate in the varied language of architecture than those who specified the full-size model village of Poundbury in Dorset not terribly far away. Where Poundbury wallows in poor pastiche, the miniatures of Little Britain were well-informed, full of wit and a spread of styles. One of the most unusual creations was 'Druid's Folly – the Contemporary House' – a very fine modernist flat-roofed home.

These villages created by Deboo and his collaborators were important structurally and commercially: not only did they start to depict urban and quite modern (rather than mainly rural or vernacular scenes) but they were a miniature empire made to make money.

Also quick to realise the commercial opportunity of a Bekonscot-by-the-sea were the Dobbins brothers, Tom, Bill and Harry. They spent time in Beaconsfield researching some of the techniques, then set up the very 1956-sounding 'Land of the Little People' in Southport. On the promenade it was described as 'For all Those who are Young In Heart' and featured the village of Merryvale (sometimes spelled Merrivale), alongside the River Merry. A model railway raced through it too, past a castle, windmills and various scenes of what we might now consider Blyton-esque tweeness. With success under their belts, Bill moved on to open up Merrivale in Great Yarmouth (1961) and Tom to Babbacombe in Torquay (1963).

The guidebook for Merrivale claimed that it 'is not just another model village... it is a typical section of the English countryside in miniature, for it has its own busy town as well as its perfectly kept village, its farm and factory, sports stadium and zoo, castles and cottages.

62561   FOUNTAINS ABBEY, EASTBOURNE MODEL VILLAGE.

A coloured postcard of Eastbourne, clearly showing the Fountain's Abbey centrepiece, the walk-through town and landscape, all held inside the Redoubt Fortress.

Margate's short-lived village on the seafront in 1970. 'Stage One' suggests that bigger things were planned beyond its two-year existence.

Over two hundred models set against a background of scenic beauty. The model trains cross the water by means of an impressive suspension bridge nearly 30 feet long, linking town and village.' But really, Great Yarmouth, Southport and Babbacombe had many similarities: the Dobbins brothers were shrewd operators and likely (sensibly) thought it pointless to invest in varied designs when a holidaymaker was unlikely to visit all three.

The late 1950s and 1960s really were the Golden Years. Forget the New Town movement: this was the postwar Model Village movement as coastal areas were almost littered with new arrivals. Cromer, Clacton,

The buildings of Lelant Model Village, Cornwall, were rather good, and made of fibreglass. They later made their way even further west, forming a cluster at the Land's End visitor attraction, after Lelant's closure. They are still there today.

Lelant model Village

IT'S A SMALL WORLD

SCALE-MODELS

MUSEUM

WATER GARDENS

Illuminated at Dusk
OPEN EVERY DAY
10 a.m. to 5 p.m.
at LELANT
(between St. Ives & Hayle)
Tel : Hayle 2676
BUS SERVICE :: CAR PARK

New County Hall, Truro, "Cornwall in Miniature", St. Agnes.   Photo: E. Nägele, F.R.P.S.

Cornwall in Miniature proudly included Truro's New County Hall. Model villages tend to include vernacular rather than modernist or brutalist architecture because of perceived romanticism and the relative difficulty of reproducing precision architecture in miniature. Thatch and cob walls are easier. (John Hinde Collection)

Did you know?

Build-Your-Own
With more people having more spare time and disposable income, magazines like *Railway Modeller* and engineering societies encouraged people to start building model railways outdoors in private gardens. Often villages followed, but usually as adjuncts to the model railways, and few survive to this day.

Southsea's walk-through nature is clear here in this 1971 view, taken in its heyday. (David Hill)

This semi-private village in Fletching, East Sussex, was small scale and arranged over several scenes, designed to be viewed over a front garden wall.

Chessington Zoo's extensive village was built, unusually, to be viewed from behind a fence, but it did mean that hundreds of thousands viewed it each year without damaging it.

'HERE COMES ANOTHER ONE!':
Model Village Railways

One of the greatest excitements for any young visitor is the surprise arrival of a model train. Not all villages have them; Wimborne, Corfe and Bourton never have, mainly because they're not appropriate for the dead-set time period or geography of those replica towns. A replica of Wimborne station, for example, would set the train tracks way over at the perimeter fence, far away from the model itself. But for other sites these trundling, careering, clickety-clacking iron horses which occasionally derail in a thrilling, clattering mess are the energy that fizz through the miniature landscape.

Model railway enthusiasts often don't take model village railways very seriously; they're seen as toys or crudely built train sets. But because, like the landscapes through which they pass, they must withstand the pressure of 1:1 scale weather and 1:1 scale hands, it is rare for them to be as detailed as their indoor counterparts. As the years pass, these railways are becoming things of real historical interest.

Bekonscot's most popular feature has always been the Gauge 1 model railway. To this day, it passes through the Maryloo Signal Box at operator waist-height for maintenance. This 1940s view shows modelmaker Bert Grey making adjustments.

One of the joys of Tucktonia was the throwing together of national icons usually separated by space and time: here a GWR steam train and British Rail Inter-City 125 pass Windsor Castle.

It is unusual for the village to match the railway scale – but then, in the mind of most visitors and builders these things are for fun rather than for accurate depiction. The scale is usually mismatched because model railways are expensive, so buying off-the-shelf or parts from manufacturers is the most practical way forward. The 1:32 railway is noticeably smaller than the 1:12 to 1:18 scale of the model buildings so the difference is lessened at Bekonscot by using transitional scales of both buildings and people at stations.

The stock from the Snowshill Manor Wolf's Cove railway (Gauge 1, 1:32 scale, built by the world-famous Bassett-Lowke Ltd) is still on display in the National Trust property. Bekonscot too was built entirely with this manufacturer's equipment. The Bekonscot railway has always been the most complex model railway open to the public in Britain, running for over 10 scale miles. Since 1929, it has been upgraded many times to include control by a real ex-British Railways lever frame from Purley signal box and, later, computer control software to allow automated running using RFID chips and barcodes.

Weymouth was unique: scaled at 7 mm to 1 foot, the railway used OO gauge track as a little narrow gauge railway; the buildings were all the same scale. Tucktonia had a fantastically extensive 2.5 in. gauge railway with several express routes, all controlled by computer, and all the stock was purpose-built.

At Anglesey, Bridlington and Belle Vue's Mini Land, the model trains really were home-built to scale; clunking along in the landscape, they are very impressive too. Stock had also been built especially for the Dobbins brothers' villages at Babbacombe, Southport and Great Yarmouth. Like all the others, it was electrically operated, and it ran in most weathers, on most days, and was built to last. Babbacombe's survives, whereas at Great Yarmouth and most other villages, the railways are now G Scale – easy to acquire off the shelf and maintain.

But the honour of most remarkable model village model railway must go to Pendon. Here, in the main indoor scale scene, hand-built locomotives of unsurpassed quality run as smooth as sewing machines, hauling trains of perfectly accurate lengths and rolling stock.

The main villages with working railways have been:

Bekonscot (Gauge 1)
Clacton (O Gauge)
Canvey Island (O Gauge)
Margate Cliftonville (Gauge 1)
Weymouth (0.16.5 Gauge)
Wimborne (OO Gauge indoor)
Southport Land of the Little People (2.5 in. Gauge)
Southport Model Railway Village (G Scale)
Great Yarmouth (2.5 in. then G Scale)
Babbacombe (2.5 in.)
Skegness (G Scale)
Llechfan Garden Railway, Tywyn (T Gauge)
Himley Hall (G Scale)

A member
of staff rights
a wrong on
Clacton's
railway circuit.
Mishaps were
frequent!

Tucktonia (2.5 in. Gauge)
Beech End, Leyburn (Gauge 1 indoor)
Godshill (G Scale)
Pendon, Oxfordshire (EM Gauge, 1:76 scale on 18 mm gauge)
Miniland Bellevue (3.5 in. Gauge)
Legoland (Large Lego Scale)
Wistow (G Scale)
Bondville (3.5 in. Gauge)
Minivale, Hornsea (G Scale)

Eastbourne, Lelant, Margate, Minehead, Porthcawl, Rhyl, St Agnes and Withernsea: give a man a promenade plot and he would have given you a tiny town. Others popped up inland, ranging from the large Chessington Zoo (one for humans and another for guinea pigs to live in – a familiar sight at several zoos over the years, including one still today at Longleat) and Miniland at Belle Vue in Manchester, down to the tiny one found at the Dumb Bell pub in Chalfont St Peter, Bucks (to keep the children quiet in the garden).

These by now had become fairly formulaic in their construction: small plots of gently landscaped gardens with concrete or rendered buildings in 1:12 to 1:18 scale, augmented by gently punning shop names, large scale model cars and buses, and a selection of figures.

Some, like Rhyl, Cromer and Margate, looked like meek incursions into a world that would punish them: flimsy looking buildings of thin render on marine plywood, perched almost on a clifftop. They didn't survive, they have gone. But in Cromer the pathways that wound their way through the trimmed grass just above the lifeboat station, at the edge of the achingly conservative North Lodge Gardens, remain. So too did, until the great storms of 2013, the lighthouse that was once in the village but was displayed on a café roof in the full-sized town. Of Margate's Cliftonville model village site, of Clacton, or Belle Vue, of Minehead – there is nothing on the ground now to suggest that they ever were. Tourism trends can be cruel.

5
Trouble in Toyland

'I will make a small fortune from this model village,' one operator told me. 'But my wife reminds me that we started with a rather bigger fortune.' As he looked forlornly across the flapping tarpaulins and puddles of a wet January. Moving into the last decades of the twentieth century, this was probably a familiar refrain.

Most history books will tell you that kingdoms of any scale take great effort to grow, but much more to maintain. In model-world, as soon as buildings are put outdoors, the elements take their toll: a lifelong war of many battles must be waged. If it is not against the elements and constant renewal of exhibits then it is against the competition of other attractions, the often flimsy loyalty of the transitory tourist audience who will move to another resort next year, or even against the planners or the bank manager. What starts as a utopia realised in miniature for many soon becomes a millstone around the neck: a world that has been created and a world that must be governed, managed, rebuilt and invested in. Life as a monarch may not be all that it is cracked up to be. Even an occasional act of vandalism can often mean the end: the capital and physical outlay to replace so much at once has often been too much to

bear. In the 1970s the tide of tourism had turned, and the visitor numbers ebbed and footfall outside front gates fell. The realisation of many original builders from the 1950s and 1960 was that they were reaching retirement age – and they wanted out.

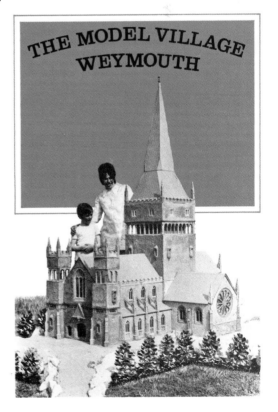

Others still tried, optimistically. Blackpool was one such and at Weymouth, Colin Sims and his wife Christine built on waste ground at Lodmoor Country Park over four years, their village opening in 1972. From stone, concrete, wood and plastics, the small-scale 1:48 village of Fendlewick grew – matching the O Gauge model railway that went with it. Fenside Junction Station was served by an automated narrow gauge railway;

Weymouth's largest structure by far was the cathedral, of independent design. Within a few years it became 'Model World', the village gaining several other miniatures not necessarily in keeping with the theme.

this 'typically British' scene was full of the typical model village puns like 'H. A. Dock' the fish merchant and Wits End Farm. Weymouth International Airport also featured, as did a fairground with 2,000 handmade parts.

The cathedral was Colin's own design – a scale 280 feet tall in concrete; it took nine months to build and was proudly displayed on the front of the brochure. It was a difficult time: hundreds of plants were set out but many died off in the salt-laden seaside atmosphere. Colin died in 1982, with Christine running it as a literal labour of love for almost thirty years,

Left: The village of Rolling Falls in Ilfracombe, Devon. Its creator can be seen centre left.
Below: Ilfracombe's 'World Models' at the edge of the town were a delicate, short-lived feature. Some buildings were better representations than others.

but the village finally succumbed to vandalism. Her son, Mark, said: 'The destruction is just senseless. My father built most of the models and they represent hundreds of hours of work.' The Weymouth buildings finally were sold on eBay and they survive in private hands.

The rural scene of Rolling Falls in Ilfracombe was a latecomer – a model of nearby Clovelly. It filled the back garden of a house in the town but alas, it was not terribly successful. It arrived just as Ilfracombe had lost its railway and the North Devon coast had lost much of its sheen. It could not survive, and the author picked his way around the husks of 1:12 scale plaster-and-wood building with the site's owner in the late 2000s.

Over in the east, Canvey Island's village finally shut in 1976, after it had moved location to the seafront and suffered several attacks of vandalism from local people. In a heart-breaking interview with the *Canvey News*, the creator's widow explained her sadness. 'I have not seen the damage,' said Mrs Fenwick, 'but my grandson has told me that everything has been completely smashed up this time. I knew I wouldn't be able to keep it going after my husband died and I tried to sell it. But it was very difficult to find a buyer. My grandson offered to run it for me and he opened for the season on Sunday. We have had so much trouble with vandals in the past but my husband was always able to repair the damage. But it is really the end of the model village now.' A similar story befell the village in the walled garden at Haigh Hall near Wigan, which had begun life as Miniland at Belle Vue in Cheshire.

Meanwhile, Southport's Land of the Little People disappeared beneath a supermarket, and the real-life Redoubt fortress that provided the home for Eastbourne's remarkably detailed village provided no protection against bulldozers. One of the council team once contacted me on Twitter to tell of his sadness at being instructed to take a pickaxe to the tiny world. Orders, of course, were orders. Lelant's model village fell by the way, as did Cornwall in

This late 1980s postcard of Ramsgate shows its charming tactility but also the general air of disrepair that had begun to set in.

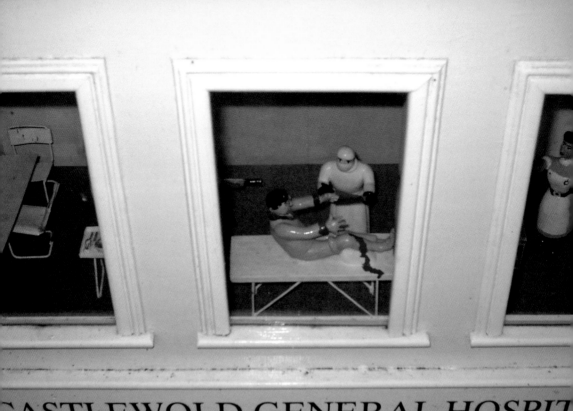

CASTLEWOLD GENERAL HOSPIT

Above: Ramsgate, in its later years, included features not immediately thought to be suitable for tiny children. (Derek Smith)
Left: A dead village: many of the remnants of Ramsgate, removed after purchase in 2003 at nearby Salmestone Grange. Some went to Great Yarmouth, some to Bekonscot and some remained locally.

Miniature at St Agnes and Ramsgate, somewhat later but after protracted failure.

We must also document the rise and fall of one of the greatest – and most missed – of all of Britain's model villages: Tucktonia, in Christchurch, Dorset. Conceived as a commercial venture, the model was a central part of the Tucktonia entertainment site which also included fairground and theme park rides. This was not the work of amateur artists: this was the work of money-makers on a mission. Alex Fisken, general manager at the time, said, 'Our complex can't rely as do many of the older model villages on the labour of love of local model enthusiasts. They might work devotedly fifty weeks a year, and then vanish for their own holidays during the very peak weeks when coach parties are unloading 60 or more people every ten minutes.'

Tucktonia was built from scratch in just eighteen months; the site was drained of water then contoured with 18,000 tonnes of hardcore and 2,500 tonnes of concrete. It was the sheer vastness of Tucktonia that made its impression. 'See Britain in One Day', the jolly ads said. And you could: you were able to stride down London streets, gawp at Nelson's Column or even stroll along Hadrian's Wall. At one point, a model of London's GPO Tower was proudly erected, assisted by helicopter.

A fabric patch for Tucktonia from 1982: similar patches were probably sewn to a fair few fur-edged anoraks of small children that autumn.

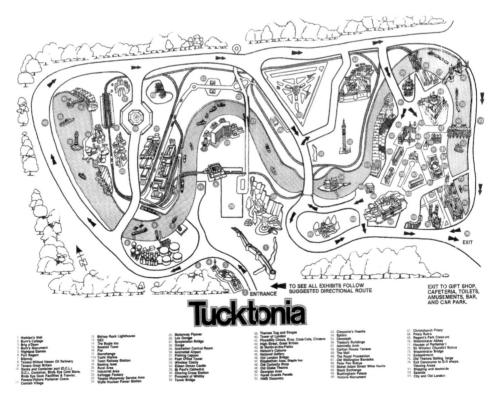

A map of the whole Tucktonia site from the second season. The extensive model railway network and varied contents can clearly be seen.

Ships moved through the rivers using steel-wired underwater channels with pulleys, rather as they do at Madurodam in the Netherlands. Tucktonia bloomed for several years, but all of the models needed replacing at about the same time. They weren't built to last – and the investment required to replace such a vast, detailed world all at once at a time of tricky domestic tourism led to its closure in 1986. Many of the models went into storage elsewhere in Dorset – but the story goes that the warehouse burnt down, taking all the models with it. All, save Buckingham Palace – stored elsewhere – which later went on display indoors at nearby Wimborne Model Town and then more recently at Great Yarmouth's Merrivale.

Tucktonia was the closest Britain ever got to a full-scale 'miniature park': a standalone paid-for attraction full of landmarks. Elsewhere, somewhat smaller in scope but still 'miniature parks', Britain has had Legoland in Windsor, an odd collection of icons in an Ilfracombe park, Paradise Park at Newhaven in Sussex, and Model World at Thorpe Park in Surrey. Model World, built to the unique imperial scale of 1:36, was positioned as a comparison of 'historical structures with those of today'. These included Pont Du Gard, the Leaning Tower of Pisa and the Eiffel Tower: many were built in steel or fibreglass and were later maintained by the Tussaud's Group Studios, the parent company which managed Thorpe Park in later years. All were removed in 2003; several including the Eiffel Tower and the Stalingrad Statue of the Motherland made their way into the author's collection. The author, on asking of the scale of the models in 2003 and being unaware,

What Makes a Village

A place without people has no soul; it is a ghost town. It is when tiny people – the wayward Lilliputians of Gulliver's Travels if you will – are added that a model village really comes to life. Those finer details are where so much of a village's character comes from. There is often contentment to be found in the scenery, interest in the architecture, intrigue and excitement in moving models, but the real joy is when the little people are put in. The opportunities for wit and (let's be honest, fairly low-adrenaline) comedy are manifold.

The cigarette-smoking pump attendant at Bekonscot always raises a smile.

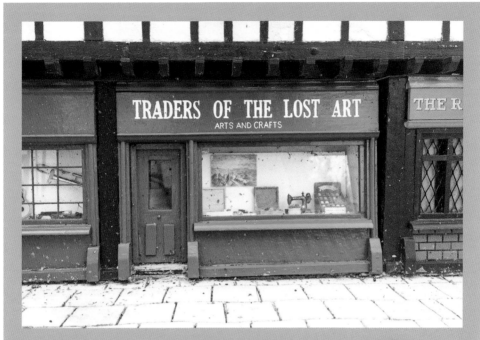

Most model villages have terrible puns. But Bekonscot has the worst.

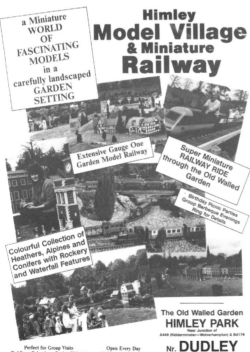

Above: Himley's model of Dudley High Street in 2003, following over a decade of closure and no maintenance. This is what happens when models are not given new coats of paint, protected or have vegetation trimmed back

Left: Himley boasted a number of scale features, including Dudley as it was in the early 1800s and even an impression of what Ambridge, the village setting of BBC Radio 4's *The Archers*, might look like.

was told that the Eiffel Tower was nine feet tall. He arrived to collect it, and found it rather larger. 'Sorry!' exclaimed the helpful team member. 'I meant nine metres, not feet!' Thus it was that only the top two-thirds of this massive model now survives in storage.

With Tucktonia 'gone on fire' and a multitude of villages closed, the map of Lilliputian Britain was looking rather bleak as the 1980s progressed.

There were some brief glimmers of hope. In 1984, a village at Himley Hall in the West Midlands opened: Fred Blakemore, his son Stuart and collaborator Bob West established Westmore Miniature Landscapes. Their 1:12 village, built almost entirely from marine plywood, occupied the gently undulating grounds of the now council-owned Hall walled kitchen garden. But the village peaked by 1989: buildings needed maintenance; the crowds never arrived to see the very competent models of historic Black Country architecture. Even the addition of a ride-on-railway and a narrow gauge tramway was not enough: this rural site closed in 1995 and by 2003 had been forgotten. The author rescued a few buildings from what had appeared become a bizzarre, post-apocalyptic world; now the site has been flattened.

Perhaps tourists wanted something more high-tech, some reasoned. So it was that an unusual indoor model village – Beech End Interactive Model Village at Leyburn, Wensleydale, was built by local businesspeople Ian and Adele Calvert. This small-scale village with controllable slot cars and trains lasted a mere seven years from 2000 and was last seen on

Did you know?

How Model People Are Made

Bekonscot's early people were carved from limewood by local schoolboys. Today the population of 3,000 people and 500 animals is made mainly from cast resin: they're created like Frankenstein's monsters from hundreds of interchangeable body parts. Larger scale villages make theirs person by person, character by character, while smaller villages often get to buy theirs off the shelf from garden railway suppliers.

One of the volunteer modelmakers at Jimmy Cauty's New Bedford delicately prepares model policemen, ahead of dozens of tiny 1:76 scale cars ready to be added to the scene.

the market for £155,000. A worthy attempt at a contemporary visitor attraction, but proof that where there is a gap in the market, perhaps there is not always a market in the gap.

Bekonscot was apparently the genesis for another little model village empire, the first of which was developed at Withernsea, in the East Riding of Yorkshire, by husband and wife Geoff and Carol Cooper. That desire – that frustration I spoke of initially to create a miniature world – was strong, and by 1965 the 1:12 world of Minivale had been opened by the Coopers to the public. A small harbourside town, where the visitor could walk along the quayside before wandering up through grassy fields and farms, was set in a small plot built up with fine concrete-shell buildings.

But this was a short-lived enterprise; ten years later the couple had packed up due to low visitor numbers and acts of vandalism. Much of the setup was moved to Hornsea Pottery, just up the coast, where a team was setting up a shopping outlet and outdoor entertainment centre. Here in 1979 the much-supplemented and rejuvenated remnants of Minivale became Minidale. A railway circuit was laid to add interest, and was quickly one of the most popular little attractions that surrounded the main pottery-themed venture.

Within a decade it was handed over to the Hornsea Freeport management team and was renamed Sleepy Hollow in an attempt to market it in a more contemporary way. But the occasional criminal act of bored vandalism, increasing maintenance costs – and, according to the site manager when the author visited in 2006, a belief that asbestos was present in some buildings – led to its closure. The author was given access then to document its cracked and hand-smashed remains and it still lies there today, behind wire mesh fences, slumbering in what now really was a sleepy hollow. I wouldn't try to go there now, if I were you.

Another town that is technically a survivor but which will likely never be on public view again is also a potentially deadly one – and it goes by the name of Tinkleford. The author spent years trying to track down the existence of Tinkleford. But it was not until the arrival of Twitter, a postcard image, a subsequent article in the *Bournemouth Echo* and an entertaining BBC Radio Solent interview that I was contacted by its current owner, Danny.

Come and see

"TINKLEFORD"

SWANAGE

MINIATURE DORSET VILLAGE (To scale)

OPEN FROM 2 p.m. TILL DUSK (weather permitting)
ENTRANCE, 1/-. Dogs not admitted.

It is easy to find. From the cross roads (Northbrook Road-Victoria Avenue) turn north up the hill and take the first turning (lane) on the left, indicated by a large arrow and poster.

An advert for Tinkleford in Swanage, before it moved from the garden of its builder to the tearoom garden. Dogs have rarely been admitted to villages for good reason!

Built in the Swanage garden of is creator, Mr Rose, these little 1:24 scale Purbeck stone, slate-and-concrete houses moved twice across the town. It went first to the Virginia Tearoom garden of Danny's parents in the 1950s, where it had a recording of the Swanage Church choir played out on a reel-to-reel among bonsai-style trees. After the tearoom's closure in 1968 the village moved again – into storage – and that is where it has been ever since until the author was shown it in early 2017.

Tinkleford has a problem. It cannot be visited. It must not be touched. For like many things of its time, it is substantially constructed from that wonder-fix-all-but-oh-god-what-monster-have-we-created material: asbestos. Today, the tiny town of Tinkleford lies in half-light on benches, with dust gently settling all around. There it must stay, until such time that it can be made safe.

Outdoors again, it was not just the villages intended for mass public view that had started to decay. Little Italy, founded by the late Mark Bourne, still (just) occupies a Welsh mountainside garden above Corris. Towering folk-art models of Italian greatness were made by this man who loved Italy so much that he decided to show local people less able to travel than him how beautiful the classical architecture was. So here exists a mish-mash of classicism and Italianate love: an Italy of the Duomo, Bridge of Sighs and a Tower of Pisa that is now leaning a little more unhealthily than its full-size cousin. It is a wonderful place: a very personal interpretation of the world, a three-dimensional postcard built at home in the Welsh mountains where reality is governed by memory alone. Concrete, steel, bits of bread oven, mannequins and detritus found in nearby quarries all help Little Italy feel like one of the great lost wonders of another world. It may not survive much longer, for Bourne is now gone and his cottage is now a holiday rental. So who will curate the art of this outsider artist now?

A coloured postcard of Tinkleford in its second home in Swanage. (Collection of Brian Musselwhite)

Little Italy's rambling collection of landmarks, built with love but falling into disrepair.

6

Pride and Preservation, Resurgence and Restoration

Many a story has a classic build-up, terrible times and then renewal of hope before a happy ending. Apparently, so runs the tale of many a model village.

Take Corfe Castle: in the lee of its eponymous ruin, the Purbeck village of Corfe Castle nestles between mound, hill and heath. The perfect illusion of a Famous Five adventure is ruined only by the twenty-first-century traffic jams, tempered only slightly by the laden steam trains of the Swanage Railway, which runs through the village.

Eddie Holland, a local businessman, had an idea in the early 1960s to differentiate his and his wife's tearoom by building a model village in it. He'd probably seen Wimborne. By 1966 he had contracted out the construction of a veritable tumulus at the bottom of the one-acre gardens, atop which was a 1:20 scale model of the castle before it was famously 'knocked about a bit' by Cromwell in 1646. Plus (obviously) a surrounding 1:20 model of Corfe village itself. Who wouldn't? Sixty-one little properties, all in concrete, were left unpainted to weather, looking rather like real Purbeck Stone, and they are arranged around extra-width streets to enable easy public access.

When Eddie died in the 1980s, his daughter leased it out, but after a lack of maintenance took it back and made some improvements. Numbers dropped. Buildings cracked. It was hard graft – perhaps not a challenge that we all would relish. After a chance written introduction, she sold it to Emily and Ed Paris in 2002.

The juxtaposition of real and model Corfe Castle is shown in this early 1970s postcard view. The trees have now grown up, obscuring this vista.

Bekonscot was not always a model of 1930s rural innocence. For many years it tried to keep up with the times: here a jet airliner is seen set to take off from what had become Hanton Airport, and later, Concorde prepares to fly.

When I first spoke to Emily and Ed in 2007, they talked of needing to make investment. I have visited several times since; the garden and tearooms are now a joy. Free croquet and quoits are available on the compact lawns; the cottage gardens bristle with blooms and the village has taken on a new life with some modern characters adding life to an otherwise 1646 scene. Concrete cracks have been filled and guests walk around, chomping on cake and supping cups of tea to fill their stomachs. In the future I look forward to seeing tiny model cannon fire on the hour, every hour, as one observer once suggested.

Edgar Wilson's little London villages (see Chapter 2) had succumbed to much damage over the years, but his jumble of chunky edifices in Vauxhall Park were 'restored' in the 1980s, and again in 2001, by volunteers. It's not much of a village now with the buildings scattered, and their lumpy nature has been enhanced by plonking each building on a paving slab. But they are painted cheerfully, and look indestructible. Brockwell Park's two remaining buildings were reconstructed too, following advice from those who helped at Vauxhall; by the middle of 2017 the concrete buildings have been added to, with the Friends of Brockwell Park planning to restore the entire scene.

Back in time: Bekonscot has now back-dated. Here is Hanton Docks *c.* 1971, and now as Hanton Fishing Village in 2017. Note the diesel trains and oil tankers replaced by steam trains and sailing boats. The latter is perhaps more saleable as a visitor attraction.

Did you know?

Some Villages Get Started, but Have Never Opened
The Pembrokeshire Model Village on the edge of Tenby was developed around 2007 and as late as 2012 had a website, but to date it still has not opened. Aerial views can be found online, showing a large scale model of the South Wales fishing town huddled around a pond, with roads as walkways.

Bekonscot too fell slightly behind the times. Its owner handed over control to the Church Army for charitable purposes and after several years of gentle repose in the 1980s, it needed complete refreshment. Riding the wave of heritage tourism, a decision was taken by its board in the early 1990s to turn back the clocks. Life imitated art imitated Poundbury. Sash windows and hanging tiles replaced pebbledash and steel. Out went Concorde and in came the biplanes. The transformation took a decade to complete: Bekonscot is now 1930s, but it is not 1930s Bekonscot. It is a fake past, a model of a model that never really was.

The visitors love it. But as visitors walk about, many of them now coming again with their children and grandchildren, they've forgotten a modernist Luton Town Hall, the aircraft hangars and the high-speed diesel trains. They see what they think they remember. It comes as a shock when, halfway around, they're presented with some then-and-now photos. Is it a real history? Can you fake the heritage of a fake building?

The handcrafted detail of Harlow Carr (now at Ryedale Folk Musum) is some of the finest of any model village in Britain. Even the hinges were fashioned by one man in a quest for perfection. Restored and renewed, this church is one of more than a dozen now on display again.

Bondville has been restored in recent years with help from its original creators, Geoff and Carol Cooper. Geoff is shown here, refacing one of the 1:12 scale cottages. (Jan Whitehead)

Smaller villages, too, in many cases saw a resurgence. A home-built village made by John Hayton over many years in his garden at Beckwithshaw in Yorkshire was donated to the RHS gardens at Harlow Carr, Harrogate, in 1986. The original volunteer team who maintained it moved on, so the team at RHS Harlow Carr approached the author in 2003 with a plea for help. Working with Anthony Coulls, a museum curator, and Stephen Levrant, a heritage architect, several sites for their relocation were identified; Bekonscot and a museum in Wales were both possible but in the end we recommended the Ryedale Folk Museum at Hutton-le-Hole. Within months the RHS and Ryedale teams had transported the entire collection on pallets from Harrogate to the Yorkshire Moors. They are now, delightfully, each restored to a high quality and seen by thousands more than they ever would be in a private garden. One man's desire to depict an archetypal Yorkshire village has now been reconstituted and renewed, given a new life and a new context. A similar story can be told in Coniston, where many carefully crafted small buildings in slate have been moved from John Usher's garden to two museum sites in the town. Semi-private has gone public, and we are all the better for it.

The Coopers, the builders of Minidale (by now languishing in Hornsea Freeport), had by 1988 developed their third village, over in Sewerby near the seaside town of Bridlington. Using many of the same construction techniques and even the same scenic layout of a quayside focal point as seen at Minidale and its precursor Minivale, an acre of grounds with tearoom were laid out. So many model village constructors have an artistic vision in their mind – an architected landscape; this village of Portminion with the slight tweaking with each site iteration clearly has been the culmination of the Coopers'. Ownership would eventually pass to the enthusiastic Jan Whitehead, who with her husband Tim was really looking for a tearoom but 'ended up with a model village too, a bonus!' They have been restoring and developing Portminion, now known as Bondville, with the assistance of Geoff Cooper too. Hundreds of miniature characters, set in poses of domestic and municipal life (that perhaps have never really existed at the same time in full-size history), are here for us to enjoy, and perhaps take solace in, while daytripping to the far east coast of Yorkshire.

Another commercial success has been Southsea, where following their mother's retirement, two brothers have taken over the village near the seafront and it is now undergoing a gentle renewal, inspiring local people to volunteer and contribute towards a project that is unlikely to make serious money again, but it will make many smile.

The 1990s saw a few new commercial arrivals. One was the Forest Model Village in the Forest of Dean. Adjacent to a garden centre and conceived as a three-dimensional tourist information point for visitors – much like Mini Europe or Miniturk – it sadly foundered within a couple of years. Its plywood buildings needed reconstruction, but as with Tucktonia, it would have been an expensive investment for very little return. A more recent indoor concept – 'Little London' – was launched with great fanfare to have become a focal point near Tower Bridge, but failed to gain sufficient investment, and at 1:148 (N gauge) scale in order to show most of Central London – would have also failed to convey much of the detail, whimsy and humour that a truly successful model village has.

Anglesey Model Village was opened in 1992 by Jim Lympany and his wife Anne. The village was marketed for sale in 2014 as a going concern, but as at early 2017, it did not seem to have a buyer. A pleasant small garden site with generously proportioned 1:12 scale buildings and matching home-built model railway, it depicted various Anglesey buildings. It was a nice site but was never going to hit the big time in that location – or indeed without the density of models seen at the more commercially successful sites.

Those commercial sites have been jumping ahead: Babbacombe with new models of the Shard and fake snow for winter (apparently a nightmare to remove in January); Great Yarmouth with new resin model houses and a new model railway; and Bekonscot with an all-time high in donations made to charity after running costs, a ride-on-railway that has carried well over a million people in ten years and dozens of refurbished or new scenes.

Those that are large have done very well; those that are small have found new ways forward through the use of volunteer labour, or by being passion projects as hobbies.

The model village at the Museum of Power in Essex has been constructed just as Fred Slaymaker's village was back in the 1950s: from scrap. Here, volunteers have assembled a toy town in an enclosure in a Womble-like fashion. A wander-through experience like Bekonscot it is not, but it is indeed a model village and a labour of love. In 2007, a new model village 'cluster' was established at the Devon Railway Centre; Matt Gicquel and volunteers have

Did you know?

There are many other must-see Lilliputian worlds in Britain that aren't quite model villages, but are worth a look.
Great Polish Map of Scotland, near Peebles
Peasholm Park Naval Warfare, Scarborough
Portmeirion Hotel and Village
Pipers Model, Guildhall, London
Building Centre Model, Store Street, London
Wroxham Miniature World, Norfolk
Rachel Whiteread's dolls' house town at Museum of Childhood, Bethnal Green

Babbacombe has continued to be successful with interactive or animated features. This postcard depicts the house on fire, with flames powered by gas and an attendant fire crew with water.

'Something terrible happened here.' The opposite of utopia: a dystopia in the near future at Jimmy Cauty's New Bedford, as displayed at Banksy's Dismaland. The stage centre-right included a hangman's noose and spotlights.

We're finishing where we started: time for a fag at Bekonscot.

similarly combined scrap, dolls' house materials and even cast-offs from what was Cornwall in Miniature, later St Agnes Model Village and even later Land's End Model Village; this collection is a smashing addition to the railway exhibits.

Edward Robinson in Cumbria single-handedly created the Lakeland Miniature Village. When I visited last, he gestured across his beautifully crafted collection of slate-hewn Lakeland vernacular, scattered over rolling hills in his front garden: 'I wanted to show the kids what went before. Real rural life. Before the barns all became barn conversions.' This village is a model of his perception. It isn't Lakeland today; it is a museum of Lakeland history. But not any old history; this is Edward's slant on history because he is depicting a scene, as in any model, where chunks of time are dismissed and he is focusing on features that he finds important.

Another of those lovely little private projects that has had wider recognition is that of Lowson Robinson, who has built several clusters of buildings in a garden in Nenthead, Cumbria: a pseudo-Big Ben sits adjacent to castles and local-style cottages, all built in Cumbrian stone. It is a joy. Even Snowshill, where it all probably began, has a new lease of life: National Trust volunteers are making replica buildings and have performed miniature archaeology on tiny foundations. In 2017 we find Wolf's Cove is rising again, and it grows with every season.

The final model village in this tale is not a utopia. It is a dystopia. A model village masterminded by former KLF band member Jimmy Cauty. 'New Bedford', exhibited indoors at Cauty's London studio and at Banksy's Dismaland, is the opposite of much of what has gone before as a rural idyll: with his team he has made an urban hell. But this dystopia for some of us is a very specific utopia for Jimmy: his vision realised in miniature because anything bigger would cost a fortune.

But still, why? Why conceive it? Why build it? Why maintain it? I have asked many a commercial and private Gulliver those questions: their answer tends to be that they don't really know. But it's because they are frustrated. They conceive, build and maintain through frustration, desire, love and then often through resignation. But we are all the better for it. We are lucky to have men and women who care, love, and share their worlds with us just to make us smile.

7
What Next?

In Chapter 1 I suggested that the aim of this book was to convince you to make another visit to a model village. Well, if you have reached this far, then you probably are going to. And if you're really keen, maybe you'll want to build your own.

Building Your Own
Some advice from a model village owner when I asked him for this book was: 'Don't.' A model village will not make you money, but it will occupy your brain, your time and your bank balance. As Jan Whitehead at Bondville Model Village says: 'To be appreciated by visitors... makes all the hard work worth doing. I have learned that owning a model village is not as easy as I once thought it would be, but the skills you learn along the way, and the people you get to meet, are amazing.'

To build a model village in the garden for occasional opening or display is really very achievable. A plot of any size – even a little front garden – has room for buildings, or a railway. What is important is the resistance to the elements: plywood will not last many seasons, but a treated wooden building frame screwed together or with cast concrete sides affixed really will. Bekonscot will espouse the sensibilities of using Foamex: a stiff foam board available in up to 30 mm thick sheets, cut by knife or saw and then having wood doors or windows inserted. Upon that, a roof made from wood and overlain by roofing felt, scored as tiles. Others will suggest individually cut bricks, stones or tiles. Others might suggest buying whole buildings from garden railway suppliers, of which there are many to be found online.

Further Research
There are not many books on model villages and the author has relied on first hand sources, village and town guidebooks, local news and magazine sources but you may find the following useful for further investigation:

Barker, Paul, *The Freedoms of Suburbia* (Frances Lincoln, 2009) – an overview of the suburban context in which many villages began.
Constable, John, *Landscapes in Miniature* (Lutterworth & Sheldon Press, 1984) – how to build a living miniature landscape on a tiny plot.
Dunn, Tim, *Bekonscot Model Village* (Jarrold, 2004) – a history of Bekonscot.
Halstead, Robin; Hazeley, Jason; Morris, Alex; Morris, Joel; *Bollocks to Alton Towers* (Penguin, 2005) - A guide to uncommonly good days out in Britain, including model villages and similar offbeat attractions.
Salter, Brian, *Model Towns and Villages In Britain In Public In All Weathers* (In House Publications, 2014) – a comprehensive gazetteer of outdoor model villages still extant.
Dolls House & Miniatures Magazine (ongoing) – mainly 1:12 scale but full of accessories and ideas for model buildings and scope to take concepts further.

There are also several websites that include points of interest:

Themodelvillager.wordpress.com – the author's own exploits.
Vimeo.com/Bekonscot – the digitised video archive of Bekonscot, including footage of various other model villages of the twentieth century.
BritishPathe.com – a remarkable trove of many miniatures, from railways to villages.
GScaleSociety.com – a group dedicated to outdoor model railways and scenery.

Model Villages on Display to the Public Today

If there are model villages that have inspired you, make a visit to one of them. They will all be glad to meet you and discuss their approach, their trials and their tribulations. Each is so different in context and construction; your best bet is to find somewhere that fits your ideal and go talk to them. Do search online for:

South West

Land's End, Cornwall
Land's End Visitor Attraction, nr Sennen, Cornwall, TR19 7AA
0871 720 0044

Polperro, Cornwall
The Forge, Mill Hill, Polperro, Cornwall, PL13 2RP
01503 272378

Torquay, Devon
Babbacombe Model Village, Hampton Avenue, Babbacombe, Torquay, Devon, TQ1 3LA
01803 315315

Corfe Castle, Dorset
The Model Village, The Square, Corfe Castle, BH20 5EZ
01929 481234

Wimborne, Dorset
Wimborne Model Town, King Street, Wimborne Minster, Dorset, BH21 1DY
01202 881924

Godshill, Isle of Wight
The Old Smithy, High Street, PO38 3HZ
01983 840364

The Model Village, High Street, Godshill, Isle of Wight, PO38 3HH
01983 840270

Bickleigh, Devon
Devon Railway Centre, Bickleigh Station, Bickleigh, Devon, EX16 8RG
01884 855671

South East

Southsea, Hampshire
Southsea Model Village, Southsea, Hampshire, PO4 9RU
02392 294706

Newhaven, Sussex
Paradise Park, Avis Road, Newhaven, Sussex, BN9 0DH
01273 512123

Vauxhall Park, London
Vauxhall Park, Fentiman Road, London, SW8 1UA
No phone (open park)

Brockwell Park, London
The Walled Garden, Brockwell Park, Dulwich Road, London, SE24 9BJ
No phone (open park)

Beaconsfield, Bucks
Bekonscot Model Village, Warwick Road, Beaconsfield, HP9 2PL
01494 672919

Pendon, Oxfordshire
Pendon Museum, Long Wittenham, Abingdon, Oxfordshire, OX14 4QD
01865 407365

Windsor, Berkshire
Legoland, Winkfield Road, SL4 4AY
08714 232 280

Whitstable, Kent (in private gardens)
101 Faversham Road, Seasalter (nr Whitstable), Kent, CT5 4BG
Tankerton Road, Tankerton (nr Whitstable), Kent, CT5 2AB

Wales, Midlands and East

Bourton-on-the-Water, Gloucestershire
Old New Inn, Rissington Road, Bourton-on-the-Water, Gloucestershire, GL54 2AF
01451 820467

Woodstock, Oxfordshire
Blenheim Palace, Woodstock, Oxfordshire, OX20 1PX
01993 811091

Wicken, Cambridgeshire (Private model village in front garden)
Near village centre. Ask in shops for directions.

Snowshill, Gloucestershire
Snowshill Manor, Snowshill, nr Broadway, Gloucestershire, WR12 7JU

Wistow, Leicestershire
Wistow Rural Centre, Kibworth Road, Leicestershire, LE8 0QF
0116 259 2009

Great Yarmouth, Norfolk
Merrivale Model Village, Marine Parade, Great Yarmouth, Norfolk, NR30 3JG
01493 842097

Museum of Power, Essex
Museum of Power, Hatfield Road, Langford, Maldon, Essex, CM9 6QA
01621 843183

Betws-y-Coed, Conwy
Conwy Valley Railway Museum, Betwys-y-Coed, Conwy, LL24 0AL
01690 710568

Anglesey
Anglesey Model Village, Newborough, Anglesey, LL61 6RS
01248 440477

Corris, Powys (Private garden on view)
Little Italy. Pathway from Corris village centre past Corris Hostel, Powys, SY20 9TS

North
Southport, Lancashire
Southport Model Railway Village, Kings Gardens, Lower Promenade, Southport, Lancashire, PR8 1XQ
01704 538001

Blackpool, Lancashire
Stanley Park, East Park Drive, Blackpool, Lancs, FY3 9RB
01253 763827

Skegness, Lincolnshire
Skegness Model Village, South Parade, Skegness, Lincolnshire, PE25 3HW
01754 228200

Grange-over-Sands, Cumbria
Lakeland Miniature Village, Winder Lane, Flookburgh, Grange-over-Sands, Cumbria, LA11 7LE
01539 558 500

Coniston, Cumbria
Ruskin Museum, Coniston, Cumbria, LA21 8DU
01539 441164

Hutton-le-Hole, North Yorkshire
Ryedale Folk Museum, Hutton-le-Hole, North Yorkshire, YO62 6UA
01751 417367

Bridlington, Yorkshire
Bondville Miniature Village, Sewerby Road, Sewerby, East Yorks, YO15 1ER
01262 410736

Nenthead, Cumbria (Private garden on view)
Village centre, Nenthead, Cumbria, CA9 3AR
No phone (garden site)

Vatnergard, Shetland (Private garden on view)
No phone (garden on site)